Legal

MW00886963

Table of Contents

Dedication

To Jon

Because he did the laundry while I wrote this book.

Introduction

I wrote this book at the request of my non-Jewish friends who wanted to learn more about Jewish holidays and thought there might be others like them who would also like to learn more.

Some of you might have been invited to join a Jewish friend for a Sabbath or Passover dinner. Some of you might be interested in learning about the holidays simply out of interest.

This book covers holidays you've probably heard of such as Passover and Chanukah. It also covers holidays you may not be aware of.

This is the second of my guidebooks for non-Jews. The first, <u>The Non-Jew's Guide to Jewish Ceremonies</u>, dealt with Jewish ceremonies such as bar mitzvahs and weddings, and this one is about Jewish holidays. If you're Jewish, you might also benefit from this book. Because I grew up in a non-observant home, there was a lot about the observance of these holidays that I didn't know, so in the writing of this book, I also learned a lot.

Whatever your reason for reading this book, I hope you'll find it informative and enjoyable.

Branches of Judaism

In order to fully understand how Jewish holidays are observed, a short discussion of the major branches of Judaism - Orthodox, Conservative, and Reform – will be useful.

Orthodox Judaism is the most religious branch, represented by over ten percent of Jews in the United States. It was the only form of Judaism prior to the 18th century. Men and women don't sit together during the synagogue services, and the services are conducted entirely in Hebrew.

Reform Judaism appeared in the 18th century and sought to modernize Judaism. Their services are mostly in English with some Hebrew and are shorter than Orthodox services. Also, men and women sit together during the services. Reform Jews represent over a third of Jews in the U.S.

Conservative Judaism is the largest branch, representing about 40% of Jews in the U.S. It emerged in the 19th century as a middle ground between Orthodox and Reform Judaism. The services vary depending on the synagogue; some are similar to Orthodox services, while others are more like Reform services. In Conservative synagogues, men and women sit together.

Members of different Jewish communities observe the holidays differently, depending on how religious they are and the different customs they observe. Those who are more religious are more likely to closely follow all the rituals and restrictions associated with the holidays, while those who are not affiliated with a synagogue may not observe the holidays at all. The rest fall somewhere in between.

Jewish holidays begin on different dates according to the secular calendar, but they begin on the same day every year according to the Jewish calendar. The secular calendar is based on the earth's rotation around the sun. The Jewish calendar determines its years according to the sun, but it determines its months according to the moon. Each month starts and ends with a new moon.

The 12 months of the Jewish calendar, their secular equivalent, and the holidays that occur during them are:

Tishrei	September-October	Days of Awe (Rosh Hashanah and Yom Kippur), Sukkot, Shemini Atzeret, and Simchat Torah
Cheshvan	October-November	
Kislev	November-December	Chanukah
Tevet	December-January	
Shevat	January-February	Tu B'Shevat
Adar	February-March	Purim
Nissan	March-April	Passover and Yom Hashoah
Iyar	April-May	Lag B'Omer (See the chapter about Shavuot)
Sivan	May-June	Shavuot

Tammuz	June-July	
Av	July-August	Tisha B'Av
Elul	August-September	

There are 354 days in the Jewish calendar. To make it equal to the 365 days of the secular calendar, a 13th month is added every few years. The extra month is called Adar Bet. This also ensures that the holidays occur during the same season every year.

When dealing with dates, this book will not use the terms B.C. and A.D. since those terms are used in relation to Jesus. Since this book discusses Jewish holidays, it will use the terms BCE (Before the Common Era) and CE (Common Era) which are non-religious alternatives for the same time periods, respectively.

All Jewish holidays begin at sunset. Generally the day you see on the secular calendar for a Jewish holiday is the full day after the start of the holiday the previous evening.

Shabbat (Sabbath)

Shabbat Explained

The Sabbath, known as Shabbat (pronounced shah-BAHT) in Hebrew, is the only holiday mentioned in the Ten Commandments. Its literal translation is "to cease," because after God spent six days on creation, he ceased. He then added a seventh day so that we could give back to Him on the day that He gave to us. The Jewish Sabbath begins on Friday night and continues until Saturday night.

In the Ten Commandments, we are told to remember the Sabbath and to keep it holy. This means not just to observe it, but to remember its significance. Its significance is two-fold – as a remembrance that God is the creator and also that He freed the Jews from their bondage in Egypt. This latter point relates to the Sabbath because in ancient times slaves were not given days off; only those who were free were allowed to rest. By resting on the Sabbath, we are reminded that we are free. It has the broader purpose of letting us be free from our daily commitments and worries.

Shabbat is the Hebrew word for Sabbath. The holiday is sometimes called by the Yiddish word Shabbes (pronounced SHAH-biss).

Restrictions

There are a number of restrictions connected to the observance of the Sabbath. These restrictions are not followed by all Jews; it depends on how religious they are.

Anything that creates something new in the physical sense is prohibited, such as cooking, writing, or igniting a fire. There are other prohibitions as well that were enacted to keep certain routine behaviors from resulting in infringements on the Sabbath. These would be activities such as engaging in business and handling money.

Simple jobs around the house are allowed, such as light cleaning or preparing meals with pre-packaged food or fruits and vegetables.

Observing Shabbat

The following is a description of what can happen on Shabbat. There are variations, depending on the religious community in which the participants were raised and how observant they are. Many less religious Jews do not observe the Sabbath at all.

On Friday night, the woman of the house will light two candles, one each for the two commandments of Shabbat (remembrance and observance) and recite a prayer. The candle lighting brings God's presence into the home; His presence is manifest in the light. A woman lights the candles because after the Temple in Jerusalem was destroyed, it was said that God is like a nurturing mother who won't abandon her children.

The family will attend a service at their synagogue lasting about 45 minutes, after which they will return home. When they arrive home, a father may bless his children, holding each child individually and kissing his/her forehead.

The family then sits down for dinner. Because cooking is not allowed on Shabbat, meals are prepared earlier and are usually slow-cooked preparations such as stews. Before eating dinner, there will be two blessings, starting with a blessing over the wine, known as the Kiddush (pronounced KID-ish). Then the Hamotzi, the blessing over the bread is said. Instead of regular bread, a braided bread made with eggs called challah (pronounced KHAH-luh) is used. (By the way, it's delicious!) Songs are sung during and after dinner. The family may recite grace after the meal, then spend time conversing or studying the Torah until it's time for bed.

The next day (Saturday) they attend Sabbath services once again, this time for about two hours, and then return home for a meal. At this morning service, a part of the Torah (the first five books of the Hebrew Bible written on a scroll) and a selection from one of the books of the Prophets are read. A different part of the Torah is read each week, so that the entire Torah is read over the course of the year.

The afternoon is spent in leisure activities, a walk, conversation, Torah study, etc. A light meal will be eaten later that afternoon.

Shabbat ends when three stars can be seen in the night sky, about 40 minutes after sundown. At this point there is a short, concluding ritual, called Havdalah (pronounced Hahv-DAH-luh), which means separation. It involves a braided candle, a box of spices, and a glass called a Kiddush (pronounced KID-ish) cup filled with wine or grape juice. Family (and friends if present) gather together, and individual people hold each of the items. There are three blessings which are either spoken or sung, one over the wine, one over the spices, and one over the candle flame. The spices are smelled by everyone, and everyone puts a hand up by the candle. There is a fourth blessing, the havdalah blessing, which blesses the separation of various things, such as the holy and the profane, light and dark, and the seventh day and the remaining six days of the week. After all the blessings, everyone takes a sip of the wine or grape juice. If there is any wine left, it is poured into a dish and the candle is extinguished with it.

Home and community are focal points of Shabbat. There is singing and celebrating at the meals, as well as studying together afterward.

The typical greeting on the Sabbath is "Shabbat Shalom" (pronounced shah-BAHT shah-LOHM), which is Hebrew for "peaceful Sabbath." Those who speak Yiddish may say "Gut Shabbes" (pronounced GUT SHAH-biss) which means "Good Sabbath."

Days of Awe - Rosh Hashanah (Jewish New Year) and Yom Kippur (Day of Atonement)

The Days of Awe Explained

The Days of Awe is the ten day period beginning with Rosh Hashanah (pronounced ROSH hah SHAH-nuh or RUSH-uh SHAH-nuh) and ending with Yom Kippur (pronounced YOHM ki-PAWR). During this period, Jews are supposed to spend their time on self-examination. They are supposed to think about the sins they have committed during the past year. On Yom Kippur they are supposed to atone for those sins. This period is also known as the Jewish High Holy Days. The Days of Awe occur in September or October, depending on when they fall on the Jewish calendar. Rosh Hashanah occurs on the first and second days of Tishrei, and Yom Kippur falls on the 10th day of Tishrei. Jews are not supposed to work on Rosh Hashanah and Yom Kippur, although they will work on the days in between. Many Jews who do not go to synagogue services any other time during the year will go on Rosh Hashanah and Yom Kippur.

Rosh Hashanah Explained

Rosh Hashanah is the Jewish New Year and celebrates the sixth day of creation when God created human beings. Its literal translation is "head of the year." Rosh Hashanah is celebrated for two days, although less observant Jews only celebrate for one day.

On Rosh Hashanah, God writes everyone's name in the Book of Life or Book of Death, indicating who, in the coming year, will live and who will die. His decision is based upon one's good and bad deeds of the past year, weighing one against the other. However, if people repent, pray and do good deeds during the next ten days, the final outcome of the books can be changed. God seals the books on Yom Kippur.

Observing Rosh Hashanah

Most Jews go to a service on Rosh Hashanah. This is true even of some Jews who aren't members of a synagogue. For observant Jews, it is one of the longest services of the year, exceeded in length only by the Yom Kippur service. The service for religious Jews usually lasts from early morning until the afternoon.

The most important ritual associated with this holiday is the blowing of the shofar (pronounced sho-FAHR) or ram's horn in the synagogue, announcing God's arrival and coronation as king of the universe. The shofar blast is also a reminder for people to repent.

Rosh Hashanah is celebrated with a festive meal at home. The following is a description of what can occur during the meal. There will be variations depending on the religious community in which the participants were raised and how observant they are.

The meal begins with a candle lighting ceremony and a blessing to God. There is also a blessing over the wine known as the Kiddush (pronounced KID-ish) and the blessing over the bread known as the Hamotzi. The table will have a braided bread made with eggs called challah (pronounced KHAH-luh) and pieces of apple dipped in honey. The round shape of the challah loaf represents the continuation of life. The apple pieces dipped in honey embody the wish for a sweet year. At the end of the meal, the "grace after meals" or birkat hamazon (pronounced BEER-kaht hah mah-ZOHN) is recited. For those who observe Rosh Hashanah for two days, this is repeated again the second day.

Greetings for this holiday include "Happy New Year" or "L'Shanah Tovah," (pronounced li-SHAH-nuh TOH-vuh), Hebrew for "Have a good year."

Yom Kippur Explained

Yom Kippur is the culmination of the Days of Awe and the holiest day of the Jewish year. It is the Jewish Day of Atonement. One asks God for forgiveness for the sins of the past year. This atonement involves reconciliation with God for sins against Him. If one has sinned against another person, one must have reconciled with that person before Yom Kippur occurs.

Restrictions

Yom Kippur is considered so important that many Jews who observe no other holiday will observe this one by going to a service, not working and fasting (if they are physically able to do so). Not all Jews who are members of a synagogue follow the fasting ritual.

Observant Jews follow other restrictions on this day, such as not bathing, not wearing perfume or leather and abstaining from sexual relations.

Yom Kippur is the only holiday that does not have room for family. Solitude is more important on this day than love, security and comfort. If you have the comfort of family, you can't feel the crushing weight of your sins. Because it's not a festive holiday, people are not wished a Happy Yom Kippur. They are wished "G'mar Chatimah Tova" (pronounced GAH-mar CHAH-TEAMAH toh-VAH) which means "May you be sealed (in the Book of Life) for a good year" and "Tzom Kal" which means "Easy fast."

Observing Yom Kippur

The following is a description of what can happen on Yom Kippur. Of course, there may be variations, depending on how observant the participants are. They may not follow all of the observances or attend all of the synagogue services.

In the afternoon before the fast begins, there is a final meal. Two candles are lit. Then there is a synagogue service. Unlike regular days which have three services (evening, morning and afternoon), Yom Kippur has five services. The evening service (remember, Jewish holidays begin at night) is known as Maariv (pronounced MAH-reev). This service includes an important prayer known as Kol Nidre (pronounced KOHL NID-ray), as well as a confession of sins.

The following day consists of a morning service known as Shacharit (pronounced SHAHKH-reet) with readings from Leviticus, the Yizkor (pronounced YIZ-kawr) memorial service for those with deceased family members or friends, and then the Musaf (pronounced MU-sahf), which tells about the Yom Kippur service in the Temple of Jerusalem. Yom Kippur is one of the four times during the year when the Yizkor service is recited (Passover, Shavuot and Shemini Atzeret are the other three).

There is usually a break after the Musaf service. The Minchah (pronounced MIN-khuh), takes place in the afternoon and is the shortest Yom Kippur service. It includes the reading of the Book of Jonah. The last service is the Neilah (pronounced n'-EE-luh). This service ends with the blowing of the shofar and the congregation shouting, "Next year in Jerusalem."

At the end of the day, people have a meal to break their fast. Dairy products are often included in this meal, as are bagels and lox (similar to smoked salmon).

On Yom Kippur, those with deceased relatives will often light a 24-hour memorial candle called a yahrzeit (pronounced YAHR-tsahyt) candle in their home.

Sukkot (Feast of Tabernacles)

Sukkot Explained

Sukkot (pronounced soo-KOHT) is one of the three pilgrimage festivals in Judaism, which means they celebrate both agricultural festivals and historical events (Passover and Shavuot are the other two). During ancient times, Jews traveled to the Temple in Jerusalem on those three holidays. After the destruction of the Temple by the Romans in 70 CE, the holidays began to be celebrated primarily for their historical aspects.

Sukkot is also known as the Feast of Tabernacles or the Feast of Ingathering. It commemorates the 40 years the Jews wandered in the desert after they left Egypt. It is also a celebration of the fall harvest. The word sukkot means booths, as in the temporary shelters the Jews lived in when they were wandering in the dessert.

Sukkot is observed five days after Yom Kippur on the 15th day of Tishrei. This falls in September or October.

Observing Sukkot

The following is a description of what can happen on Sukkot. There may be variations depending on how observant the participants are. They may only follow some of the rituals, or they may not follow any at all.

The holiday is observed for seven days by Israelis and many Reform Jews. It is observed for eight days by other Jews living outside of Israel. For observant Jews, no work is done on the first two days.

There are three practices associated with Sukkot – building a sukkah (pronounced SUK-uh, it's the singular of sukkot), dwelling in the sukkah and waving the "four species."

On Sukkot, observant Jews build a sukkah, which is basically a temporary hut covered with vegetation and decorated with autumn vegetables. The Bible commands that people dwell in their sukkahs. Some sleep in them, while others simply eat in them. Some people build their own, while others buy prefabricated ones. In some communities it has become customary nowadays for synagogues to build a sukkah for the community to share, rather than having individuals build their own.

It is customary for Jews to invite others to share a meal with them on Sukkot. Tradition states that Abraham, Isaac, Jacob, Moses, Aaron, and David are on hand in every sukkah.

Another Sukkot observance involves the arba minim or four species. These are fruits and branches used to fulfill the commandment to "rejoice before the Lord." A palm branch, two myrtle branches and three willow branches are tied together. Holding them in the right hand and holding a citron (a citrus fruit found in Israel) in the left hand, a blessing is recited while waving them east, south, west, north, up and down. This is to represent that God is everywhere.

A common greeting on Sukkot is "Chag Sameach (pronounced KHAHG sah-MEHY-ahkh) which means "joyous festival" in Hebrew.

Shemini Atzerit (Eighth Day of Assembly) and Simchat Torah (Joy of the Torah)

Shemini Atzerit Explained

Shemini Atzerit (pronounced sh'MEE-nee aht-ZE-ret) takes place on the eighth day after Sukkot, the 22nd day of Tishrei. It commemorates the beginning of the rainy season after the harvest in Israel and is a time to pray for rain. This is because crops that were planted in the spring rely on the rain that comes in the autumn.

Some people believe this day is a part of Sukkot, when in actuality it is a separate holiday. Even if people sit in the sukkah on this holiday, they do not say the prayer that is normally recited there.

Observant Jews do not work on this day. Shemini Atzerit is also one of the four days of the year that Yizkor, the memorial prayer for departed relatives and friends, is recited in synagogue (Yom Kippur, Passover and Shavuot are the other three).

Simchat Torah Explained

Simchat Torah (pronounced SIM-khat TOH-ruh) celebrates the importance of the Torah in Jewish life. It is the time when the reading of the Torah in synagogue is concluded and started over again at the beginning. The holiday is a celebration during which the Torah scrolls are carried around the synagogue seven times. Members of the congregation hold banners and sing Hebrew songs while the scrolls are being carried.

Among Conservative and Orthodox Jews outside of Israel, the holiday occurs on the ninth day after Sukkot, the 23rd day of Tishrei. Among Reform and Israeli Jews, Simchat Torah is celebrated the same day as Shemini Atzerit.

A common greeting on Simchat Torah is "Chag Sameach (pronounced KHAHG sah-MEHY-ahkh) which means "joyous festival" in Hebrew.

Chanukah, Chanuka or Hanukkah (Festival of Lights)

Chanukah Explained

Chanukah (pronounced KHAH-nik-uh), or the Festival of Lights, is an eight-day celebration of a miracle that occurred in 165 BCE. An outnumbered Jewish army, led by Judah Maccabee, fought and was victorious over the Syrian-Greek army that controlled Jerusalem and oppressed the Jews. There was only enough oil to light the Temple menorah (pronounced m'-NAW-ruh), a seven-branched candelabrum, for one day; however, it miraculously lasted for eight days, the amount of time needed to prepare additional oil. Chanukah falls on the 25th of the Hebrew month of Kislev, which usually occurs in December, but may occur in November.

Observing Chanukah

Chanukah is considered a minor Jewish holiday, because it doesn't have a lot of restrictions associated with it. Unlike most other holidays, it is not celebrated in a synagogue. It is celebrated at home with family.

In celebration of the miracle with the oil lasting eight days, candles are lit in a Chanukah menorah, for eight nights. A Chanukah menorah, unlike the Temple menorah, has a place for eight candles instead of seven. There is also a place for an additional candle known as the shammus (pronounced SHAH-mis) that is used to light all the others. The shammus candle is set apart from the others, often by height. Each night one more candle is added to be lit. The candles are placed in the menorah starting on the right side and added from right to left.

On the first night of Chanukah, one lights the shammus candle and uses it to light the first candle on the right. On the second night of Chanukah, the shammus candle is used to light the first and second candles on the right. The newest candle is lit first, so although they are added from right to left, they are lit from left to right. This continues for the eight nights of the holiday until on the eighth night, all the candles on the menorah are burning. Each night when the candles are lit, a blessing is recited. The candles are left to burn themselves out.

Greetings for Chanukah include "Happy Chanukah" and "Chanukah Sameach" (pronounced KHAH-nik-uh sah-MEHY-ahkh) which also means "Happy Chanukah."

Giving Gifts

Giving gifts was not traditionally a part of Chanukah. Some say it was added in the 19th century as the Christmas season became more commercial in tone and Jews began to live in communities with non-Jews. Before this time however, it was traditional to give Chanukah gelt (Yiddish for money). One explanation for this is it recalls ancient times when Jews were independent and allowed to mint their own coins. Another is that in the Middle Ages, Jewish teachers were given money as a gesture of appreciation. Eventually it became the custom to give coins to children as an incentive to learn until they were old enough to understand the importance of education.

Chanukah gelt is often still given to children, in either real or chocolate-covered candy form.

In Israel, it is not customary to give Chanukah gifts. If any gifts are given, they are usually candy, Chanukah gelt or dreidels (pronounced DRAY-d'ls) (see the section on Playing and Singing).

Food

Fried foods prepared with oil are eaten as an acknowledgement of the miracle of the oil lasting for eight days. Potato latkes (pronounced LAHT-kuhs), which are potato pancakes, are popular in the United States, and jelly-filled doughnuts are a common treat in Israel.

Playing and Singing

Some celebrate Chanukah with songs and games. A popular game is the dreidel (pronounced DRAY-d'l) game. A dreidel is Yiddish for spinning top. This game originated during the Jews' oppression by the Syrian-Greeks. Because the Jews were not allowed to study the Torah, they would play games with a top to hide their studying whenever an official came around.

Each of the dreidel's four sides has a different letter. They are the first letters of the phrase, "Ness Gadol Haya Sham," which means "Great Miracle Happened There." This refers to the miracle of the oil lasting eight days.

Why Are There So Many Spellings?

There are many different spellings for Chanukah. I've just shown three of them in my chapter title. The reason given for this is that the English spelling is just an approximation of the Hebrew pronunciation. The first sound is like "kh" and has no similar sound in English, so some use a "ch" and some just use an "h". Sometimes two "k"s are used in the final syllable to give it extra emphasis. Sometimes only one "k" is used.

Tu B'Shevat (New Year For Trees)

Tu B'Shevat Explained

Pronounced TOO bish-VAHT, this minor holiday is known as the New Year for Trees. Although it occurs in January or February (15th of Shevat on the Jewish calendar), it is associated with the start of spring in Israel. This is when the some trees begin a new cycle of producing fruit.

The original purpose of the day was to determine the age of trees for harvesting and for tithing at the Temple in Jerusalem. On Tu B'Shevat, farmers offered the first fruits from their trees at the Temple when those trees turned four years old. The farmers were allowed to use those trees for personal or commercial use on the following Tu B'Shevat.

After the Temple was destroyed by the Romans in 70 CE, the holiday was observed by eating fruits and nuts that are native to the Land of Israel.

In the middle ages, Kabbalists (those involved in Jewish mystical activity) introduced a Tu B'Shevat seder, similar to a Passover seder. It involves eating fruits and nuts that can be found in the Land of Israel and drinking four cups of wine.

Observing Tu B'Shevat

Since the start of Zionism in the 19th century, settlers in the Land of Israel planted trees to turn the desert into a fertile land. This activity on Tu B'Shevat grew into a tradition. People living in other countries often donate money for the planting of trees in Israel. So the holiday is one of planting trees and celebrating the rebirth of the Jewish homeland.

There are no restrictions against working on this holiday. There are also no required special meals or prayers. However, it is traditional to eat from the seven species, fruits and grains mentioned in the Torah as the main produce of the Land of Israel. A blessing is said if this is the first time during the season one is eating any of these fruits. The observance of this tradition is dependent on how religious the participants are.

Some Jews have started to attach an ecological significance to this holiday, linking it to our responsibilities to preserve the planet. They have reintroduced the Tu B'Shevat seder to reflect these issues.

There is no specific greeting for this holiday.

Purim (Feast of Lots)

Purim Explained

Purim (pronounced POOR-im) is a holiday that celebrates the saving of the Jews from annihilation at the hands of the prime minister to the King of Persia (known as Iran today) in the 4th century BCE. It comes from the word Pur, meaning lots, because Haman, the prime minister, drew lots to determine which month to destroy the Jews. Purim is considered a fun and joyous holiday because the Jews were triumphant over Haman.

The story of Purim is told in the Bible in the Book of Esther. Esther was a beautiful Jewish woman who lived in Persia. She had been raised by her cousin Mordecai, the leader of the Jews. Esther was chosen by King Ahasuerus, the king of Persia, to become his queen, but under advice from Mordecai, she kept her Jewish identity a secret from the king.

When Mordecai refused to bow down to Haman, the latter went to the king. The king left the fate of the Jews in Haman's hands, and Haman decided to exterminate them on a date chosen by a lottery. Esther was persuaded by Mordecai to speak to the king on behalf of the Jews. Esther asked Mordecai to have all Jews fast for three days, and she fasted as well, in preparation for her meeting with the king. She invited King Ahasuerus and Haman to a banquet in which she told the king of Haman's plot. The king ordered Haman to be hanged and gave the Jews the right to defend themselves against their enemies. On the 13th of Adar, instead of being killed themselves, the Jews fought and were victorious over many of their enemies. Esther and Mordecai declared that they should celebrate on the next day.

Observing Purim

Purim is considered a minor Jewish holiday because it doesn't have a lot of religious restrictions. It has become significant because the story has resonated with Jews throughout their centuries of anti-Semitism and survival.

Purim usually falls in February or March. On the Jewish calendar, it falls on the 14th of Adar everywhere except in Israel. In Israel, the holiday is celebrated on the 15th of Adar and is known as Shushan Purim. The reason for the difference is that the Jews of Shushan continued fighting their enemies through the 14th of Adar and celebrated on the 15th, while others fought only on the 13th and celebrated on the 14th. Israeli Jews identify with the Jews of Shushan. Although Purim is not a major holiday, it is widely celebrated in Israel with street festivities, parades and costumes.

Observant Jews traditionally fast on the day before Purim. This is done in remembrance of Esther asking Mordecai to have all Jews fast for three days on her behalf before she met with the king. After this fast, the fun of Purim begins.

Observing Purim involves attending synagogue to read the Scroll of Esther, also called the Megillah (pronounced m'-GILL-uh). Before the reading begins, three blessings are said. During the reading, whenever Haman's name is mentioned, people will boo and shake noisemakers in order to drown out his name. After the reading, an additional blessing may be said.

Children and adults may attend the reading of the Megillah dressed in costume. Traditionally, they would dress as characters from the Purim story. Nowadays however, many tend to wear Halloween costumes. The wearing of costumes stems from Esther's initial hiding of her Jewish identity from the king.

Many synagogues also hold Purim carnivals with booths, games and food. They also perform skits called the Purim shpiel (a Yiddish word pronounced shpeel) parodying the Book of Esther. These have evolved beyond the Purim story to include contemporary community and world leaders.

Jews are supposed to eat a festive meal on Purim. It is called Seudat Purim, and it is eaten on the afternoon of Purim. This meal encompasses an atypical amount of lightheartedness and drinking of wine. According to the Talmud (the collection of Jewish law and tradition), one is supposed to drink until he doesn't know the difference between "cursed is Haman" and "blessed is Mordecai." The drinking of wine highlights the portions of the Book of Esther that involved drinking of wine, such as Esther planning a banquet for the king and Haman during which she disclosed Haman's plan for the Jews.

Nowadays many people have become more aware of the problems of alcohol abuse, so excessive drinking on Purim has become less popular in some communities. Others interpret the call to drink as simply getting tipsy rather than completely drunk.

A traditional food eaten on Purim is called hamentashen (pronounced HAH-men-TAH-shen), a Yiddish word meaning "Hamen's pockets." It's a tri-corned cookie filled with fruit, chocolate, or poppy seeds. The Hebrew word for these cookies, oznay Haman, means "Haman's ears." You can see what hamentashen look like in the photo on this chapter's cover.

It is also customary at Purim to give to the needy and to friends. The former, called Matanot Laevyonim, traditionally involves giving charity to two needy people. Giving food to friends is called Mishloach Manot. This typically includes a beverage, fruit, or hamentashen, but any ready-to-eat food is acceptable. Traditionally, two different foods are given to one person.

At Purim, people say "Happy Purim or "Chag Purim Sameach" (pronounced KHAHG POOR-im   sah-MEHY-ahkh), which means "Happy Festival of Purim."

Pesach (Passover)

Pesach Explained

Passover, known as Pesach (pronounced PAY-sahkh) in Hebrew, is the holiday that celebrates the ancient Israelites' freedom from slavery in Egypt. The story is told in the biblical Book of Exodus. God caused 10 plagues to be rained down on Egypt before the pharaoh would agree to grant the Israelites their freedom. Those plagues were blood, frogs, lice, beasts, cattle disease, boils, hail, locusts, darkness, and the death of the firstborn sons of Egypt. The Israelites marked their doors with lamb's blood so that God would know to "pass over" their houses and not kill their first-born sons.

The Israelites were led out of Egypt by Moses after which the pharaoh had a change of heart and pursued them. God parted the Red Sea, allowing them to cross. When the Egyptians entered the parted sea, God closed the pathway through the sea, and the Egyptians drowned. The Israelites wandered through the desert for 40 years until they reached the Promised Land.

Passover occurs in March or April. On the Jewish calendar, it begins on the 15th of Nissan. It lasts for either seven or eight days. Reform Jews and those living in Israel observe Passover for seven days. Conservative and Orthodox Jews outside of Israel observe the holiday for eight days. This difference has to do with the fact that holidays are determined by a lunar calendar and in ancient times, the beginning of a new lunar month was determined by observation of the new moon in Jerusalem. People who didn't live in the Land of Israel added an extra day to their holiday just in case they were wrong about the date of the new moon.

Passover is one of the three pilgrimage festivals in Judaism, which means they celebrate both agricultural festivals and historical events (the other two pilgrimage festivals are Shavuot and Sukkot). During ancient times, Jews traveled to the Temple in Jerusalem on those three holidays. After the destruction of the Temple by the Romans in 70 CE, the holidays began to be celebrated primarily for their historical aspects. Passover celebrates the exodus of the Jews from Egypt and the start of the new spring planting season.

Restrictions

The Israelites left Egypt in such a hurry that they didn't have time to prepare. They didn't have time for the dough of their bread to rise, so on Passover, Jews eat unleavened bread called matzo (pronounced MAHTZ-uh).

During the days of Passover, Jews are not supposed to have any leavened product in their homes and must clean remnants of these products from their stoves, refrigerators and cooking utensils. They can best avoid eating forbidden foods by only buying those labeled "Kosher for Passover." Many observant Jews have special dishes, utensils, and pans that are used only for Passover.

Observing Passover

The following is a description of what can happen on Passover. Of course, there may be variations. Depending on how observant the participants are, they may not follow any or all of the rituals.

Jews are not supposed to work on the first one or two days and the last one or two days of the holiday. Again, this varies by how religious one is. Only about 10 percent of American Jews strictly follow this rule.

The day prior to Passover, firstborn males are supposed to fast. This is done in remembrance of the fact that the firstborn sons of the ancient Israelites in Egypt were not killed.

The religious service for Passover is conducted at home and includes a meal. This ritual dinner is called a Seder (pronounced SAY-d'r) and is held on the first night and sometimes again on the second night.

The Seder is read from a book called a Hagaddah (pronounced huh-GAH-duh). The Hagaddah is centuries old, but there have been many versions published since the original. They all include the telling of the Passover story (the exodus from Egypt), blessings, instructions for the Seder, and explanations of the Seder's symbols. These symbols are all placed on a Seder plate. Before describing the Seder, it's important to understand what is on the Seder plate.

The Seder Plate

There is one Seder plate per table, and it holds six foods:

Zeroah, a shankbone representing the blood from a lamb the Israelites put on their doorposts so the angel of death would pass over their houses. Some communities use a chicken neck instead of a lamb shankbone. Vegetarians use beets.

Baitzah (pronounced BAYT-sah), a hardboiled egg. There are several interpretations given for this. One is that it symbolizes an offering brought to the Temple in Jerusalem in ancient times. Another is that it is a symbol of mourning for the destruction of both the First Temple (by the Babylonians in 586 BCE) and the Second Temple (by the Romans in 70 CE). A third explanation is that its round form represents life and death. Finally, some say it is a symbol of spring, the season in which Passover is celebrated.

Maror, a bitter herb, usually horseradish, representing the bitterness of bondage.

Charoset (pronounced kha-ROH-set), a blend of fruit, wine, almonds and cinnamon, representing the mortar the ancient Israelites used to make bricks. There are several different recipes for charoset.

Karpas, a green vegetable, usually parsley, symbolizing the Israelites' first years in Egypt when they thrived before being enslaved by the pharaoh. The vegetable is dipped in salt water or vinegar to symbolize the tears the Israelites shed when they were slaves.

Chazeret (pronounced khah-ZER-et), romaine lettuce, representing a second portion of bitter herbs, eaten as part of the Hillel Sandwich (See number 10 in the section describing the Seder).

The Seder

The Seder has a number of parts that are set out in the Hagaddah in a particular order. Depending on how religious the participants are, not all parts are done during the Seder. Therefore, the Seder may be as short as 15 minutes (not including the dinner) or as long as a few hours. The parts are briefly described below:

1. A blessing is said over the wine and everyone drinks from their glass. Sometimes grape juice is used instead of wine, particularly for children.

2. Water is poured over everyone's hands as a symbol of purification. The water is poured over the right hand first, then the left hand.

3. A vegetable is dipped in salt water and eaten. As explained above, this represents the tears shed by the ancient Israelites during their bondage.

4. During the Seder, there is a plate holding three pieces of matzo. The person conducting the Seder takes a piece from the middle and breaks it into two pieces. The smaller of the two pieces is put back, and the other piece is wrapped in a napkin and becomes the "afikomen." After the Seder, the afikomen is either hidden by the leader and hunted by children for a reward, or the children "steal" the afikomen and the leader rescues it with a reward.

5. The story of the exodus is read from the Haggadah. The youngest person at the Seder reads the Four Questions. The questions all revolve around the question, "Why is this night different from all other nights?" Other Seder participants will read the answers to the questions aloud from the Hagaddah.

The Four Questions deal with the following:

1. On other nights we eat all kinds of bread; why on Passover do we only eat matzo? (Because our ancestors left Egypt in such a hurry, they did not have time to let the dough on their bread rise.)

2. Why, on this night, do we only eat bitter herbs when on all other nights we eat many herbs? (To recall the bitterness of our ancestors' bondage in Egypt.)

3. Why do we dip our food twice on this night when we don't dip it even once on other nights? (The salt water into which we dip the karpas (green vegetable) symbolizes the tears of the ancient Israelites when they were slaves in Egypt. The dipping of the bitter herbs into the charoset symbolizes the mortar they used to create the bricks for building.)

4. Why on this night do we eat while reclining, when on other nights we sit in any position? (Because free people reclined in ancient times, and our ancestors became free on this night.)

After the Four Questions, four types of children are described – the wise child, the wicked child, the simple child, and the one who doesn't know how to ask a question. This allows for introspection and conversation.

Another cup of wine is poured and the 10 plagues of Egypt are read out loud. Seder participants dip a finger into their wine and place a drop onto their plates as each plague is read.

The food on the Seder plate and what each one represents is discussed, after which everyone can drink their wine.

6. Those around the table wash their hands again. This time a blessing is said.

7. The generic blessing for bread and grains is recited over the matzo. Then a specific blessing for the matzo is said.

8. The Seder participants eat their matzo.

9. A blessing is recited over the maror (the bitter herb representing the bitterness of bondage). It is then dipped in the charoset (the blend of fruit, wine, almonds and cinnamon) and eaten.

10. Next, participants make what is called a Hillel Sandwich, maror and charoset between two pieces of matzo.

11. Dinner is eaten next. There are no special requirements for the meal other than the one regarding no leavened food. Many Jews begin the meal with matzo ball soup (chicken soup with dumplings made from matzo meal, water, eggs and chicken fat or shortening) and gefilte fish. Roast chicken, turkey and beef brisket are common entrees.

12. After dinner, the afikomen (see no. 4) is returned to the person leading the Seder and eaten by the participants.

13. A blessing is given over a third cup of wine before being drunk by everyone. A fourth cup of wine is poured, including one for the prophet Elijah. The door to the home is opened for a while for Elijah to enter. Another reason given for opening the door is

that historically Jews were accused of putting the blood of Christian babies in matzo, so they left their doors open to show that this wasn't true.

14. The door is closed. Everyone sings songs and recites psalms and drinks the final cup of wine.

15. A final blessing is said which in English translates to "Next year in Jerusalem," the wish that next year Passover will be celebrated in Israel or that the Messiah may come within the next year.

There are several greetings that are used on Passover, such as "Happy Passover," "Happy Pesach," and "Chag Pesach Sameach" (pronounced KHAHG PEH-sahkh sah-MEHY-ahkh), which means "Happy Passover" in Hebrew.

An Additional Passover Observance

Although the main religious observance for Passover is the Seder which is conducted in the home, religious Jews may also attend synagogue services. During one of these services, Yizkor, the memorial prayer for departed relatives and friends, is recited. Passover is one of the four times during the year when this prayer is recited (Yom Kippur, Shavuot and Shemini Atzeret are the other three). Some people also light a 24-hour memorial candle called a yahrzeit (pronounced YAHR-tsahyt) candle in their home.

Yom Hashoah (Holocaust Remembrance Day)

Yom Hashoah Explained

Holocaust Remembrance Day is called Yom Hashoah (pronounced Yohm ha-SHOW-ah) in Hebrew. It is a new holiday that was established by the Israeli government in 1953. The day commemorates Jewish resistance to the Nazis between 1933 and 1945. It falls on the 27th day of Nissan which is in March or April on the secular calendar. This date was chosen because the Warsaw Ghetto Uprising occurred at this time. If this date falls on the Sabbath, the holiday is moved to the prior Thursday or the following Monday.

Because this is a new holiday, there are no traditional activities, such as fasting, associated with it. Many communities hold commemorative events.

Observing Yom Hashoah

Many observe this holiday by lighting memorial candles and saying Kaddish, the prayer for those who have died. There may be a variety of events in different communities such as prayer services in synagogues, educational programs in schools, and talks given by survivors.

Yom Hashoah is a national holiday in Israel. On the night before the holiday, there is a state ceremony at Yad Vashem, Israel's Holocaust memorial. The day of the holiday at 10:00 in the morning, air raid sirens blare. Israelis stop whatever they are doing, including driving, to think about and pay their respects to those who died in the Holocaust. Public places of entertainment are closed and flags are flown at half mast.

Shavuot (Festival of Weeks)

Shavuot Explained

Shavuot (pronounced shuh-VOO-oht) is also known as the Festival of Weeks. It celebrates the giving of the Torah (the first five books of the Hebrew Bible, known as the Five Books of Moses) at Mount Sinai. Shavuot means weeks and it occurs seven weeks after the second day of Passover. According to the Torah, it took 49 days for the Jews to travel from Egypt to Mount Sinai, so the fiftieth day is celebrated as the day that the Torah was given. The 49 days between Passover and Shavuot are known as the Omer (pronounced OH-mayr) and are counted out loud every day during a special blessing in evening synagogue services.

The Omer has traditionally been considered a time of semi-mourning, although the reason for this is not clear. Some site a plague, or possibly a battle, that killed 24,000 students of Rabbi Akiva (one of Judaism's great scholars) during an Omer in 130 CE. Whatever the reason, traditional Jews do not get haircuts or throw weddings or parties during this period, with the exception of the 33rd day of Omer. That day, called Lag B'Omer, is considered to be a minor holiday since that is the day the plague is believed to have ended.

Shavuot is one of the three pilgrimage festivals in Judaism, which means they celebrate both agricultural festivals and historical events (the other two pilgrimage festivals are Passover and Sukkot). During ancient times, Jews traveled to the Temple in Jerusalem on those three holidays. After the destruction of the Temple by the Romans in 70 CE, the holidays began to be celebrated primarily for their historical aspects. Shavuot commemorates the giving of the Torah at Mount Sinai as well as the harvesting of wheat and fruit.

While many people call the holiday Shavuot, you may also hear some call it Shavuos (pronounced shuh –VOO-iss).

Observance of Shavuot

Shavuot observances may vary depending on how religious the participants are. Jews are not supposed to work on this day. It is traditional to stay awake all night and study the Torah. One reason given for this is that when the Jews were given the Torah by God, they didn't get up early enough, and God had to wake them up. Another explanation is that it represents Jews' commitment to the Torah and that they are always prepared to receive it.

The Ten Commandments are read in synagogue on this holiday. Also, the biblical Book of Ruth is read. There are several reasons given for this. One is because Ruth and her husband were King David's great, great grandparents, and King David was born and died at this time. Another is that Shavuot is a harvest festival and the story takes place at harvest time. Yet a third explanation is that Ruth was a convert to Judaism, and on Shavuot all Jews were in a sense converts because they accepted the Torah and its teachings on this day.

It is customary to eat dairy products on Shavuot, although the reasons for this vary. One possibility is that when the Jews were given the Torah, they became obligated to follow the kosher laws (avoiding eating dairy and meat dishes together). Another is that it represents Israel, known as the land of milk and honey.

Because Shavuot is a harvest festival, some people decorate their homes and synagogues with fruit, flowers, foliage and aromatic spices.

Shavuot is one of the four times during the year when Yizkor, the memorial prayer for departed relatives and friends, is recited. (Yom Kippur, Passover and Shemini Atzeret are the other three).

A common greeting on Shavuot is "Chag Sameach (pronounced KHAHG sah-MEHY-ahkh) which means "joyous festival" in Hebrew.

Tisha B'Av (Jewish Fast of Av)

Tisha B'Av Explained

Tisha B'Av (pronounced TISH-uh BAHV), also known as the Jewish Fast of Av, occurs on the 9th day of Av on the Jewish calendar. It is a day of fasting and prayer to remember various events that occurred on the 9th of Av. Three such events were the destruction of the First Temple in Jerusalem by the Babylonians in 586 BCE, the destruction of the Second Temple in Jerusalem by the Romans in 70 CE, and the destruction of Jerusalem in 136 CE. The day also observes other tragic times in the history of the Jewish people, such as their expulsion from England in 1290 and their expulsion from Spain in 1492.

The 9th day of Av on the Jewish calendar occurs in July or August on the secular calendar. The holiday cannot be observed on the Sabbath, so if it falls on that day, it will be observed on the 10th day of Av.

Observing Tisha B'Av

The observance of Tisha B'Av may vary depending on how religious the participants are. There is a three-week mourning period leading up to Tisha B'Av that begins on the 17th of Tammuz. On that date in 70 CE, the Romans began ransacking Jerusalem. Observant Jews do not get married or participate in celebrations during this period.

Nine days before Tisha B'Av, a more intense mourning period starts. Orthodox Jews do not eat meat, get haircuts, wash their clothes or participate in fun activities such as movies or dancing.

There are a number of restrictions to observe. One should refrain from eating (unless health restrictions apply); washing, shaving, wearing cosmetics; wearing leather shoes; and sexual activities. Work is permitted, but some prefer to not work. Torah study, which is considered pleasurable, is not allowed except for the Book of

Lamentations, Job and parts of Jeremiah. Some very religious Jews sleep on the floor using a stone under their heads as a pillow.

The meal eaten before the fast begins includes round foods such as eggs or lentils. These foods symbolize the life cycle and therefore are eaten when in mourning according to Jewish tradition.

In synagogue, members of the congregation may sit on low benches or on the floor. The Book of Lamentations, about the destruction of the First Temple, is read, and mourning prayers are said. Also, the ark where the Torah is kept is covered in black. Because people are in mourning, they don't acknowledge one another with greetings.

For More Information

If you would like to read about any of the topics in this book in more depth, here is a list of websites to check out.

Branches of Judaism

http://www.shofarbetzion.com/01/thethreebranchesofJudaism.htm

http://www.templesanjose.org/JudaismInfo/history/jewishbranches.htm

http://projectinterfaith.org/page/judaism-guide

http://en.wikipedia.org/wiki/American_Jews

The Hebrew Calendar

http://judaism.about.com/cs/hebrew/f/calendar_lunar.htm

http://www.chabad.org/library/article_cdo/aid/526874/jewish/The-Jewish-Month.htm

Shabbat (Sabbath)

http://www.jewfaq.org/shabbat.htm

http://www.myjewishlearning.com/practices/Ritual/Shabbat_The_Sabbath/Shabbat_101.shtml

http://www.myjewishlearning.com/practices/Ritual/Shabbat_The_Sabbath/History/Rabbinic_I.shtml

http://www.kveller.com/traditions/Shabbat/shabbat-basics.shtml

http://www.jewfaq.org/havdalahref.htm

Days of Awe – Rosh Hashanah (Jewish New Year) and Yom Kippur (Day of Atonement)

http://www.jewfaq.org/holiday2.htm

http://www.jewfaq.org/holiday3.htm

http://judaism.about.com/od/holidays/a/roshhashanah.htm

http://www.myjewishlearning.com/holidays/Jewish_Holidays/Rosh_Hashanah/At_Home.shtml

http://www.myjewishlearning.com/holidays/Jewish_Holidays/Rosh_Hashanah/Themes_and_Theology/Book_of_Life.shtml

http://www.jewfaq.org/holiday4.htm

http://judaism.about.com/od/holidays/a/What-Are-Jewish-High-Holidays.htm

http://www.infoplease.com/spot/yomkippur1.html

http://www.chabad.org/holidays/JewishNewYear/template_cdo/aid/177886/jewish/What-is-Yom-Kippur.htm

http://www.jewfaq.org/holidayg.htm

Sukkot (Feast of Tabernacles)

http://www.jewfaq.org/holiday5.htm

http://judaism.about.com/od/glossary/g/sukkah.htm

http://urj.org/holidays/sukkot/

http://urj.org//holidays/sukkot//?syspage=article&item_id=3381

Shemini Atzeret (Eighth Day of Assembly)/Simchat Torah (Joy of the Torah)

http://judaism.about.com/od/simchattorah/a/all_8atzeret.htm

http://www.myjewishlearning.com/holidays/Jewish_Holidays/Shemini_AtzeretSimchat_Torah/Shemini_AtzeretSimchat_Torah_101.shtml

http://www.hebrew4christians.com/Holidays/Fall_Holidays/Shemini_Atzeret/shemini_atzeret.html

Chanukah, Chanuka or Hanukkah (Festival of Lights)

http://www.jewfaq.org/holiday7.htm

http://www.chabad.org/holidays/chanukah/article_cdo/aid/605036/jewish/Chanukah-FAQs.htm

http://www.myjewishlearning.com/holidays/Jewish_Holidays/Hanukkah/At_Home/hanukkah-gifts.shtml

http://www.bhg.com/holidays/hanukkah/traditions/hanukkah-history-traditions/

http://newsfeed.time.com/2011/12/20/why-hanukkah-is-the-most-celebrated-jewish-holiday-in-america/

Tu B'Shevat (New Year for Trees)

http://judaism.about.com/od/holidays/a/tubshvat.htm

http://theshiksa.com/what-is-tu-bshevat/

http://hebrew4christians.com/Holidays/Winter_Holidays/Tu_B_shevat/tu_b_shevat.html

http://www.chabad.org/library/article_cdo/aid/465904/jewish/More-on-Tu-BShevat.htm

Purim (Feast of Lots)

http://www.jewfaq.org/holiday9.htm

http://www.chabad.org/holidays/purim/article_cdo/aid/645309/jewish/What-Is-Purim.htm

http://urj.org/holidays/purim/101/?syspage=article&item_id=60400

http://www.myjewishlearning.com/holidays/Jewish_Holidays/Purim.shtml

http://www.touristisrael.com/purim-in-israel/4965/

http://www.hebrew4christians.com/Holidays/Winter_Holidays/Purim/purim.html

Pesach (Passover)

http://www.myjewishlearning.com/holidays/About_Holidays/Types_of_Holidays/Pilgrimage_Festivals.shtml

http://www.britannica.com/EBchecked/topic/303554/Jewish-religious-year/34912/Pilgrim-festivals

http://www.chabad.org/holidays/passover/pesach_cdo/aid/871715/jewish/What-Is-Passover.htm

http://judaism.about.com/od/holidays/a/passoverdays.htm

http://www.jewfaq.org/holidaya.htm

http://www.jewishvirtuallibrary.org/jsource/Judaism/holidaya.html

http://judaism.about.com/od/holidayssabbath/f/seders_two.htm

http://judaism.about.com/od/holidays/a/What-Is-A-Passover-Seder.htm

http://www.chabad.org/kids/article_cdo/aid/1608/jewish/The-Seder-Plate.htm

http://www.chabad.org/holidays/passover/pesach_cdo/aid/1998/jewish/The-Seder-Plate.htm

http://judaism.about.com/od/holidays/a/sederplatesymbols.htm

http://www.happypassover.net/4-questions.html

http://www.chabad.org/holidays/passover/pesach_cdo/aid/511100/jewish/Answers-to-the-4-Questions.htm

Yom Hashoah (Holocaust Remembrance Day)

http://www.timeanddate.com/holidays/jewish/yom-hashoah

http://history1900s.about.com/cs/holocaust/a/yomhashoah.htm

Shavuot (Festival of Weeks)

http://www.jewfaq.org/holidayc.htm

http://www.myjewishlearning.com/holidays/Jewish_Holidays/Shavuot/Shavuot_101.shtml

http://www.chabad.org/library/article_cdo/aid/2156/jewish/Learning-on-Shavuot-Night.htm

http://urj.org/holidays/shavuot/

http://judaism.about.com/od/holidays/a/countingtheomer.htm

http://www.hebrew4christians.com/Holidays/Spring_Holidays/Sefirat_HaOmer/sefirat_haomer.html

Tisha B'Av (The Fast of Av)

http://www.timeanddate.com/holidays/us/tisha-b-av

http://www.myjewishlearning.com/holidays/Jewish_Holidays/Tisha_BAv/Rituals_and_Practices.shtml

http://judaism.about.com/od/holidays/a/tishabav.htm

http://www.jewishfederations.org/page.aspx?id=80490

Meet Elizabeth Reynolds

Hi! I'm Elizabeth Reynolds, author of the best-selling book, <u>The Non-Jew's Guide to Jewish Ceremonies</u>. I've now written this new book, <u>The Non-Jew's Guide to Jewish Holidays</u>, at the request of some of my non-Jewish friends who wanted to learn more about those holidays.

Whether you're a non-Jew looking to learn more about the Jewish religion or a Jew who, like me, grew up in a non-religious Jewish home, I think you'll find my "guidebooks" packed with information about the Jewish culture.

I've been married to a non-Jew for 18 years, so I've had abundant experience in explaining Jewish holidays and customs to my husband's family. I hope you will find my books enriching and enjoyable.

I'm also the author of <u>Are You Ready to Be a Substitute Teacher? Practical Tips for Keeping Your Sanity.</u> Working as a substitute has been fun, rewarding, annoying and wearisome - sometimes all in the same day. In this book, I share my experiences so you'll be able to find more of the positives and fewer of the negatives that can accompany the job of substitute teacher.

Other Books By Elizabeth Reynolds

If you enjoyed this book by Elizabeth Reynolds, you may also enjoy her other books:

The Non-Jew's Guide to Jewish Ceremonies

and

Are You Ready To Be A Substitute Teacher? Practical Tips For Keeping Your Sanity

21202901R00037

Made in the USA
San Bernardino, CA
09 May 2015